In Praise of Hotel Rooms
and other poems

Also by Fiona Zerbst

Parting Shots (Carrefour, 1991)

the small zone (SnailPress, 1995)

Time and Again (UCT Younger Poets Series/SnailPress, 2002)

Oleander (Modjaji Books, 2009)

In Praise of Hotel Rooms
and other poems

by

Fiona Zerbst

DRYAD PRESS

People! Read Poetry

In Praise of Hotel Rooms
and other poems

Dryad Press (Pty) Ltd
Postnet Suite 281, Private Bag X16 Constantia, 7848,
Cape Town, South Africa
www.dryadpress.co.za
business@dryadpress.co.za

Cover design and typography: Stephen Symons
Editor: Michèle Betty
Copy Editor: Helena Janisch

Set in 9.5/14pt Palatino Linotype
Printed and bound by Digital Action (Pty) Ltd

First published in Cape Town by Dryad Press (Pty) Ltd, 2020

ISBN 978-1-990936-55-5

Visit www.dryadpress.co.za to read more about all our books and to buy them.
You will also find features, links to author interviews and news of author
events. Follow our social media platforms on Instagram and Facebook to be
the first to hear about our new releases.

for Derek and Karen Shirley and Ruan Botha

CONTENTS

I

II

III

I

In Praise of Hotel Rooms

That hush behind curtains
you can't describe later:
a hotel's anonymous
shuffling of bodies, the cool, bland
surfaces lovely as rest homes,
fresh-paint complete.

I love oval tables,
blonde wood, deep-set lights,
bedspreads drawn back
like a fan's tasteful opening, scent
of corridors, acres
of sleep – like deep woods.

I harbour a vision
of animals grazing, at grass in the same
timid place, untroubled
by predators. These are the fields
of silence and pillows –
dream-sated, yielding to sheets.

Tools

Tired, as I am
of useful words –
words like tools,
blunted, numb,

stupid with sheen
and mallet-heavy –
still I come
to lay them out

row after row,
used before,
honest with use,
or stunted, solid,

rusted, worn,
dull as a hoe.
Pared them down
in dry acceptance,

worked them
to some kind
of useful blankness:
all glamour gone.

Driving Through the Karoo

Ridged acres of nothing and heat,
the meat of a dog's gum. In the Karoo,
salt-burnt skies and outcropped rock

invite a vision. Once, years back,
on a train through the same terrain, you saw
a mountain lettered with fire. Now

you're driving, gargling words like tooth-
brush water, seeing broken rock,
not wings or palms. There is no balm

for a grazed, weather-worn land, as dry
as a farmer's hand. It's all survival
now; there's nothing left of the child

you were and yet you try, persist –
your stunned and sunburnt movement
still the site of it all, that freckled, heat-

plated, sheep-defined Karoo of the mind.
Knuckling these pebbles of words
alive, you pray. You drive.

Circles

There are places where you choke on heat.
Where rock, stripped of its fat,
is muscle used up.
Where sheep lie flat
like drawstring bags in the sand.

You have to move on, to go.
Find water, shreddings of meat,
light or a house on a smudged hill
where people, asleep on their feet,
gain simple refuge.

You had it once:
a hand that opened, let go,
because you were older, old enough
to explore those charred remains,
the circles of *Inferno*.

Plateau

~ Rustenburg, 2010

Rust and rock,
that clenched enclosure,
a decade done.

I have made
these hills my life:
oh, pitiless

unregarding heat;
oh, metal
in the vein.

I have been hot
with vacancy,
volcanic fire

crusted with
grass, evasion,
a frill of glass.

This is my home.
Noon sparks,
a timid vagary.

Language

We heard the lioness calling cubs
through early evening silence.
Her nameless language – grunt
and cough – was almost like despair
and echoed in darkness there.

Then the silence that decides
our fates. How much less was later
said in our own words as we lay
and listened to untranslatable gargles,
faint through a kill's thick hide.

On the Chilean Border

The shore sand lightened
on Chile's border,
as if the boundary
were real; reeds
touched green water lightly;
pine trees shaded
the snow-stroked mountains.

I thought of running
the border, fugitive,
past the workmen
in earth graders, dull
officials with hands like putty.
I thought of heading
into that wilderness

where the lake bent
like a horseshoe,
while an unpainted, broken bench
and the Virgin's shrine
were all that kept
the post intact,
the border from sinking.

On the edge of two split-
infinitive countries,
I tested my silence against
the silence. Language
of lake, snow, cliff.
All my life I'd longed
for such freedom

from awkwardness.
No day went by
I did not think
of breaking away,
of trying my hand
at some other life,
making a dash

for the forest beyond.
I'd kept in mind
that point, Santiago,
the brutal full stop
where one language,
one life, could end
and another begin.

Photographing Preah Kahn

~ Cambodia, 2004

Remember the light at Preah Kahn,
a temple that's been left intact,

which is to say been left in ruins.
Remember the irreducible fact

of light on stone, on fallen stone.
A banyan tree whose massive roots

covered the roofs and galleries.
The places where you lay to shoot

the temple's halls, the apsaras
who dance forever on broken walls

as if the span of centuries
has been as nothing. Darkness falls,

claims the hidden jungle where
some animals hunt and others wait,

while men and women crawl away
from the massive, shadowy gate.

Landscape with Crows

They flew low, symmetrical wingspans
dark, lovely harbingers
of storm air, lifting the greyish, coppery
clouds, turning in lazy motion
over the four-lane highway
as our car headed towards
the winter evening (ridged hills
cold as fish gills).

If there was light, it wasn't easy
to see it, but I sensed it on
the underside of life – a ditch
of contrasts, where cloud and shadow,
wet marsh and rising crows
(the hum of life beyond
the stalled traffic of my thoughts)
were enough to hold me in

the pitch and roll of motion,
on the edge of storms.

Electrical Wire

Sheep stand miserably
in the mottled field,
where chalky rocks
are darkening with rain.

A watery, metallic
light on the underside
of drifting grey clouds
shifts as the water

in the tin-grey river
breaks into fragments.
Thin-voiced mosquitoes
rise above the gash

of land where darkness
keeps the muddy bubbles
from our consciousness.
We walk across the grass

now streaked with damp,
where chunks of earth loosen,
fall in on themselves,
and darkness runs

like electrical wire,
loose, down the hill,
longing to connect
with water's widening pool.

After-Image

Big, ungainly, dog-like,
it ran across our path,
vanished into the dusk,
which absorbed it silently,
the way a rock
absorbs the rain.

The after-image
of that huge, dark animal
flickers in me
when I want to describe
a thought that's gone –

because of the doubtful
spark that I am,
which barely holds up
as the bushveld night
comes on.

Knysna Seahorse

Herringbone-fine,
this bristly corpse
of a seahorse is
a baby, half-

thumb-sized,
its fluted snout
poking out,
now petrified.

Seen head-on
it's barely there,
a skinny figure
by Giacometti,

space half-whittled
away from nothing –
and yet it
floated once

in the shallow lagoon
with vertical grace,
in the seven veils
of surrounding salt,

a suturing place.

Mythology

Roosters irradiate the dawn. Come day,
this is my reminder, this is my gauge,
and everything follows. Dipped sky, pale
enclosure of grasses. Trees standing quiet.
Early summer. You cannot speak

but what bold voices call from the dark?
What mythological coming sees you
rigid, stricken, holding your heart,
as if something bears up from the bowels
of the earth, to rise all red in your open beak?

Presentiments

I remember this chunk of coast,
its lace-and-honeycomb cliffs,
cream lengths suffused with pink
and fringed with light. I recall

the houses dozing, blinds down
on windows, rattled pods, a breeze
that brought the grass to light.
And heather gone to amber

in evening's thatch of darkness.
The rich beads of a mouse's eyes
in shadow. And between us –
this line of coast and me –

that dried-out puzzle of salt
on a maze-like path of sand.
A chunk of coast in a crescent
where at last I came to rest

after years of loneliness,
presentiments of death.

Flight

Almost upside down
in the aluminium plane
he built with his hands –
the *Sling*, he named it –

we circled low above
Orlando Towers where
a bungee jumper leaped,
embracing gravity.

Bouncing around in
a seemingly fragile
tin-can cockpit while
accelerating rapidly

towards the sun,
we grabbed the edge of sky
that hot November day
(I had to close my eyes).

James flipped it over
easily, and we fell
towards the wetland
stretching to the edge

of the city. A river
shattered into miracles
of light as he righted
the plane to end

our flight at Tedderfield.
While driving home
along the highway,
I remembered gulping terror,

somersaulting delight.

After Loss

I look for you in threaded strings
of rivers, or the blast of wind
through rocks; the sober cloud that forms
and darkens so the angels can't

descend. That line of stones and pines
radiating from crumbling clouds
reminds me of the day we spent
close to each other's panting breath

along the path. In losing you,
I've lost whole tracts of land – unfenced
inheritance – and gained the darkness
of this day that presses in

like rain that blots the horseshoe bay.
All I hold is words and shells,
fragments of the lonely moon
whose craters cannot fill themselves.

The Emigrant

~ for Ali Belgasime

Libya squats on your life
like one of its Roman ruins.

You can't escape its labyrinths,
the white dust of its towns.

Obsessed with heat and death,
you smoke, forget to eat.

Your efforts come to nothing.
You sleep, you dream of times

before your father died,
his truck trashed on the road

to Tripoli. His face
unmarked in death, at peace.

The Making of the Carpet

It was made in Balochistan, by hand,
where sky is dry, like sand. Heavy

with reds and tawny thread, it was rolled,
a saddle of sorts, for an old man on a camel.

Over the stones, pebbles, dusky roads,
dustier by the hour, it was held at borders

on night routes out of Balochistan.
Look at it – centre of gold and ivory,

warm as light, blue and aubergine
fringing the white and gold where you touch it.

Know it could fly, this carpet, over
thrice-nine lands where princes lie waiting,

the seller said, his fables wry
on his tongue. Its pedigree may be dubious:

brown threads, greased wool, knots, the whole
knuckled lot woven indoors, but fashioned

out of light like chipped sky. Look at it, here:
midnight warmth of a tangerine flower,

honeyed, giving its fragrance to the air.
It becomes the colour these fingers made,

miraculous, fresh, unseen before.
Like the gasp of life, like sudden blood

that feeds a vein: amazing, amazed; life
that is suddenly possible anywhere.

Chinese Box

Of an afternoon, you can catch
the clasp of this lacquered Chinese box:

trace hexagonal dragons over
the edge, or fix a pattern of thread

that's meant to be fire, always blooming
out of the curls of pearl-polished snouts...

When those dragons glide off the lid,
they scratch against you, claws in your fingers,

breath in your hair. One afternoon,
they'll slide into you, giving you fire.

This is no myth: you're scratched and singed,
spattered with red. Though you've hidden

them once again – that box on a high shelf –
you could still find them. *Ecstasy. Dread.*

Normal

When I was twelve,
I saw on an old-style bus
in the transport museum
the ghost of a man who'd died.
He seemed to call –
so I turned to look.

He was sitting on a seat
at the front and staring
with the saddest eyes
I've ever seen.
He wasn't quite solid;
I could see the lines

of the seat he was on.
When I got home,
I told my mother
I'd seen a man
who I thought was dead,
but she wasn't fazed,

she wasn't fazed one bit.
I've seen them at
the foot of the bed,
people who've died;
family members, she said –
and she isn't one

of those mystical types
you meet who go on
and on about things
like the afterlife.
She's down to earth
and wears floral dresses

and loves to play *Scrabble*.
These things happen,
so don't be afraid,
don't be afraid,
it's perfectly normal.

Normal. Take it as read.

Hemingway: A Note

Clouds above a sea: part green, part white,
as if an island rose into the sky
to hover, shaken palm trees on their sides,
or heads. The fish are running, as they did
when you would set your pen against the tide
and let the words, like blood, seep on their own,
out of your wounds. Not that you'd say
if they were fresh. All that you saw was sea,
uncomplicated islands, morning silence.
Then you'd watch the sun rise over Cuba,
settled in the sand, your heart, or somewhere.

La Recoleta, Buenos Aires

Like a suburb I'd never seen,
its damp and empty streets a maze,
La Recoleta drew me in
among the dead, where silent days

go on unchanged. The feral cats
crouched in the drizzle, under trees,
their pointed faces quizzical
between urn base and marble frieze.

They gazed at me. I gazed at them.
It was just one of those days
when everything slows to symmetry
and even mute things amaze.

The dead seemed present. What decays
are week-old roses, history, time.
I walked among the rows of tombs,
their sills thickly layered with grime.

Imagined bones, thousands of bones,
trapped in time, or falling fast:
an hourglass of minutes, seconds,
draining unstoppably into the past.

One Night in Kyiv

Renting a shabby apartment for
the night was illicit, furtive – we would
catch a woman's eye at the station,
follow her into the street, make sure
that nobody else was following.
Her frame would lean away from us
among the traceries, frosted leaves
of evening. In the end, we'd reach

a block of flats in that city of grand
illusions. That was just how it was
in Kyiv. Later, desperately cold,
we'd walk until we came across
a glass-fronted restaurant – tiny place
that longed to be French. We'd stand a moment
under the chestnut trees, then cross
the street. A vehicle smashed into

the trunk of an oak. Drunk, the occupants
ran off. It was not far, from there,
to the centre of survival, where
we'd savour *myaso pa francuzski*,
drink vodka in the smoke
and gold of a telescopic evening
there in Kyiv, high above
a dream of planets – way back when

a little money was fine, enough;
when we were young and still in love.

Odessa Days

Walking down Tchaikovsky Street
perhaps some twenty years ago,
you thought you'd always love the man
who brought you here, who loved you so…

You weren't much good matrimonially:
refused to cook and didn't do much
but sulk at the window, homesick for
a familiar life in your faraway country.

You've moved on now, as people do.
The past's rich promises are as dust,
years outstripping memories.
Pushkin's quite inscrutable bust

squats on a shelf, with photographs
of flower sellers, Potemkin's steps
and all the history grown beyond
(once delightful, strange and new).

The opera house, the cobbled streets,
grandmothers dressed in funereal black –
all representing grief and loss,
the days of youth we never get back…

Highway 60 Corridor

~ for Whitney Gillis Zylstra

Whitney and I are pumping gas
in a suburb in Toronto, headed for
the lakes and pines, the solitary hikes
that middle-aged women take to review

their lives. The world is passing us along
like down-river logs – we leap and flail
in a vision of the future hard to accept,
and yet there's this: mist and leaf-loam;

cabins built to withstand the ice;
mountains broken on themselves,
shining in frost. The world can pass
to the young, the unconcerned – we

drive on anyway, noticing chickadees
readying for winter, plump and sleek.
Maple leaves are coming into red
and rain is washing through Muskoka's coves

ahead of the Highway 60 Corridor.
We can smell the still-hidden lakes
as we head as far north as we can go,
far from our families, from our lives,

on to Canoe Lake and the clasping
pine trees massing up against the sky.
A full moon rises above the water –
here, where autumn settles down to die.

The Endling

The Tasmanian tiger or thylacine is one of the most fabled animals in the world.
– Parks & Wildlife Service, Tasmania

Tiger-dog marsupial,
nobody knew what to make of you,
held in a tiny cage
in perpetual splayed awkwardness,
long nose pointing
into the diamond wire.

You were the end-striped endling
that fell from history's pages
in 1936, your pouch
and yawning jaws mere oddities
(jaws too weak to kill sheep,
though bounty hunters disagreed).

It may be that your kind
lives on – naturalists believe
the elusive Tasmanian tiger (or wolf)
still walks among us,
hovering between myth
and evidence of scat.

Yet we have these photographs
of you, the last, the final one –
they show you much like any other
prisoner: lying
in the heat, or standing
at the fence, as if
awaiting commutation
of a sentence.

II

The Bay

~ in memoriam Stephen Watson

I

There, on the shore, those broken rocks
fragment the light and shade. I see you
on the sand, waving faintly
from that other side, where life
seems a mirage in dimming green –
your face now clear, not seen-unseen,
because I am awake. The sea
offers up waves in which you wade
until you're almost solid again,
alive within the poems you made.

II

You loved that bay. It glitters, of course,
with grey-tailed fish in swilling green,
a foaminess that brews in the sun
above a wave that runs without breaking.
Salt air at morning, salt at night,
the fires of air and light that become
this moving place. Your shade stood here
and said to me: watch darkness come.

III

What words for those of us now left?
We crowd around ourselves, measure
our shadows fretfully, like children
growing up too fast but feeling
small. What words for the friend
you were, the light you offered walking
by the sea? Your face half-gone
in memory surfaces, clear, in dreams.

IV

To write is to cry, or cry out, perhaps.
To wait for the burning horizon to tinge
to duskier darkness, less outraged.
Leaning into the words that have bled
upon the page, I'm offering up
the notion that writing may not be
what saves us: curse of a dimming
consciousness hurtling to a dead end.

V

Do I leave you here, or visit again?
When the doors unlock and the keys fall rusted,
what comes in? I've tried to escape
the inevitable, falling away
from holding everything tight, too tight.
Now looking up at the vanishing sky,
I imagine dying. Words are as nothing.
One keeps on writing. God knows why…

VI

A line of the lightest foam teases
water out, slowly, bubble by bubble.
Only the pink sand shows to us
its underdone, helpless colour.
What's out of reach is going away,
leaching into a washed-out past.
Do I follow you, line-inch by line-inch,
where waves pour into themselves?

III

The Hotel Room on the Second Floor

The hotel room on the second floor
had views of the infinite – the sea
expanded into everything
and everything was dark in me

like waves that turn the evening in.
I almost sensed the wooden floor
resist the weight of us. The stairs
creaked and swayed defensively

in the hotel room on the second floor.
Empty bookshelves held the air
in shadow. Windows framed us there
as if we'd nowhere else to go.

Such was our loss, our final weeks –
you on the stair and I below.
All's gone silent, cold and strange
in time's imperilling flow.

Small

Two weeks after her father had died,
she watched the neighbour's kids on bikes
go up and down the driveway.
The TV spoke in a kindly voice,
seemingly from another room
or galaxy, its steady familiar
speech just like the non-stop waves
she remembered lapping against a beach,

keeping her calm as she tried to sleep.
She couldn't sleep, but took no pills
(she hated them), focusing instead
on dark rectangles in the room.
Then light (the kind you sometimes see
through telescopes) came spilling through
the curtains. Kids were sounding false
alarms in sing-song voices on

the next-door drive – tired, bored,
waiting for Christmas – while she lay
inside and watched the ceiling fan
move hot air around and around;
as she lay cocooned in pain,
recalling how her father's voice
would sing her into sleep. Never
would she feel that lost, that small again.

Song for the Body

Do you have time for the body,
its fevers and shaking strings,
its longings held and knuckled
beyond a scoop of cravings?

This is not home but makeshift:
the world laid flat, a truck stop
for the body's low vibrations
before a long, hot journey.

Can you avoid the shavings,
abrasions, lines of sight,
these pillows, boards of bone?
Presumably it's final

as an infant's first abandonment.
Where do you go from there?
Cradle your given language
in the telephone of your hair.

Three for Raymond Carver

I *Poems don't matter that much*

Poems don't matter
that much. Language
hooks itself, a fish, to a stray line
caught on a rock, accidentally.

Look. Gutted because that line
was there in the first place,
taut, abandoned,
finished, messy, after the fact.

Poems. They only come
after you've tried living.

II *The stagnant river*

Have a look at the river
for a while. Heavy and green,
gone swamp-like, thick
with algae. If you stand here, soon
you'll hear a fish jump.

Then the rump
of green-wet rock will dumb
again, the willows
hang. It's like a painting.
Nothing moves. Until it does.

Unless it is
your eye that leapt
along a line, discovering
a fish turned over, numb,
but still alive.

Keep watching.

III   *On reflection*

I came to the land
with my own cropped silence
notched in me,
like a tree one marks
one's shade on.

Here, where the land
gives heat, marks time,
mirrors of rivers
hang upside down,
a silence I can live in,

listening. Waiting.

I Find No Solace

There is no tinsel in the soul.
This is a desperate, lonely time.

Poor folk don't end up in the tales
of Russian writers, and the snow

is bleak on the window, barely festive.
Europe slips on ice, and slides

on history's darkness. Hunched birds
are motionless on a frozen river.

Migrants walk beneath a shred
of moon. I haven't the time to see

how this will end, or if these stones
will speak from ruins. On the whole,

I find no solace, even in lines
of other writers, but what is true

is the poetry of Greek tragedians,
who loved beauty as much as we do.

June

is icy, ungainly,
weighs too little
but still seems heavy;
hangs in a handful
of berries in the veld,
their dark-red
poison spilt.

Somehow, your body
can't stop trembling;
can't find the future
by moving along,
yet can't sit still.
So you push beyond
the lonely site

where once you stood
enclosed in dark,
undone in veld,
a place of ash
and fragile sky,
a suite for the damned.
The river coughs

out silt and shivers
beyond the season.
It's spiteful, June –
it will not end,
and cannot close
as it wades
among its memories.

Kafue, Zambia

I

Grass shifts and murmurs
with soft clicks, living language,
breeze across the vlei.

II

Waterbuck approach
the outpost of my silence.
Freeze, or look away.

III

Breeze wafts through the tent's
mesh. Song of painted reed frogs
lost for a moment.

The Dead

Therefore, don't despair if you see death. Nothing really dies.
— Ben Okri, *Astonishing the Gods*

The dead, who watch
with half-closed eyes,
appear as lizards on leaf walls,
vein-disguised.

Coiled in green,
their half-smiles dipped
in gold leaf, lying
somewhat despised

at the outpost of being,
they watch us, without
touching the earth.
As if they had crossed

oceans of air and capsized.

Portrait of Three Lions

Huge-pawed, cautious,
headed for the shreds
of kill: two cubs,
a lioness.

Black-tipped ears and tail:
a luminous negative.

They trudge until the scent comes.
The muzzle of one is
browned with blood,
that of the other with rouge.

Around them, light
is flattening, going.
We sit a metre
away and watch.

Just six months shy
of outright abandonment,
the cubs act up, impress
the passive lioness.

They do not know
how hard it's going to get:
that raw inheritance.
Rictus of kills
remembered, in a donga.

We watch them play,
now stronger for the feed;
then we mark the moon,
those threatening hills.

Campsite, Pilanesberg

~ for Ingrid Andersen

Disinherited bats
leave this camp to sodium lights
and woodsmoke.

Our makeshift homestead
offers rusks and speech
bubbles up to the air.

Outside, in the park,
leopards, knowing hunger,
seek a casual kill.

Inside, campsite politics –
furtive grins,
competition for the lawns.

Meanwhile, full moon
shows a huddle of kills,
frills of antelopes' bones.

Safe here, we brew fresh coffee;
recite new poems.

Surfacing

Ibises siphon through stalks of stiffened grass,
frogs burble somewhere below the willows,

winter leaches from the branches as they darken.
In the sap of new words, you're like this river

as it flows past trampled clumps of grass and reeds.
A single hoopoe parades his rust and black about

the edge – now here, now lost among the grasses,
now in relief against the corduroy of trees.

You belong to this: you dive into the river
to find what's lost, to be a part of moving things,

plunging deep into the circuit of the water,
surfacing like a fish-devouring fledgling.

On the Edge of Darkness

We live on the edge of darkness,
accustomed to the brooding veld,
abraded aloes, pellets of kudu,
hills that are sliced into silence.

This deepening shelf of place:
a cave becomes a den for brown
hyenas. When it's cold at night,
we hear their echoing shrieks

(the stars bleed out, as if they have
been half-chewed). We stay alert
for other signs: bones and ash,
tokens of language, fallen leaves.

Present Continuous

Morning weeps. The dew is everywhere,
thick on leaf and petal. In the air,
tiny flies, newly hatched, are salad green
and sticky, their wings attracting to their sheen
the morning's handout of perpetual light,
its spit-wet, warm, intractable, slight-
est radiance. Birds offer meaningless cries.
The night's permitted language slowly dies
with brightness coming up. The day invades
the crevices of body, mind. These shades
of history's continuous, afterthought past
are captured in photographs, hoping to last
beyond the hour of these upturned faces,
purple-shadowed morning glories.

Closer to Light

Days were wet as dew-touched hedges;
that year, though, there was no dark leach
of light from huddles of orange berries.
They burnished quickly.

Then October was moist with sunlight:
long, pale silence of Sundays, though
he did not come. But that was no longer
a thorn in your side and nothing

was torn from the green hedge.
You suffered lightly; you went
to the edge of yourself and saw that,
over time, the wounds could heal.

You came to yourself and knew
that even jasmine, tossed in wet wind,
opened at last: those light-starred flowers,
that heady scent.

The Black Sea

I remember it cold and trimmed
with long, white strands of jellyfish.

It quivered in sunless torment,
shelving dark waves to show

long, deadly trails of shadow.
I chose not to swim or dive.

I poked the horizon with a stick,
raised a storm from the Bosphorus.

When I drive to the sea, I think
of that poisonous time when healing

should have come, and didn't;
healing should have come, but didn't.

Near Odessa

Above the Black Sea, on the cliff,
you stand alone where poppies wave
their fiery centres at the sun,
where Ovid's exile stranded him.

It's Pushkin who's the sentry here,
although it's not his shade that hovers,
homesick, as the sails of ships
inflate with wind and head for Turkey.

What you have: loose coins, the change
of a clattering language, and the fear
you feel when staring at the waves,
much deeper than your dying here.

You still see bleached and eerie strips
of drying seaweed washed up there
on sand and pebbles; spread out like
the remnants of a dead woman's hair.

Summer on the Dniepr, Ukraine

A river waterlogged with time
was clogged by water lilies

at the edges; it was hard to drop
down into brackish water where

they spread and fattened in the heat
of summer days of wondering

whether or not the Dniepr had
polluted us with radiation…

The dacha was a fortress on
the far horizon. We would sleep

for afternoons in a bobbing boat
beneath the hanging willow trees.

Fish never took the waiting line –
they had it made in murky water.

Burnt, we swam, until at last
we headed for the wooden house,

twilight waiting with berry jam,
green mosquitoes whining. As

we set the chessboard up, we saw
swallows from the fading west

come to reel the insects in,
busy themselves with half-built nests.

The great beyond had shown its hand:
a fading sky, its rust and orange

giving up its blush and glow.
The river holds me down, within.

Healing is years away, of course,
and not a place I think I know.

Unnamed Libyan Town, 2012: A Photograph

At first, I didn't know this place,
bent like a postcard from an older
century. Crinkled, sepia.

I saw a column in the sand.
An abandoned tank, a tired flag.
A water bottle, empty.

This was the full stop of a place.
All the commas before had dropped
from our tongues and pages,

leaving this:
a bullet casing
and a jammed stopcock.

Losses

Morning's unexpected losses:
petticoats of throw-off leaves;
the love that cannot be given again.

After the Air Show

~ for Omar Hamed

We were left staring at silent engines,
the landing strip scuffed and empty;

skulked by the fence, where crushed
cigarettes and cactus plants had formed

a collage on the apron. You revealed
your life in Iraq as an engineer

maintaining government planes. You said:
There's really no margin for error when

an aircraft's up there. It's not enough
to simply do your best. You walked

beside me as we left the airfield,
eyes flicking towards the hangars,

looking for clues. I have no words
for what you've lost – the enormous cost –

but I've felt how tailwinds of the past
unsettle, capsize the future.

Kung Fu

The ladies of Chut Sing Tong Long
would sit on the roof and dangle their feet
from the gutter in 'Made in China' shoes.

They'd smoke, chew gum and joke around
as they watched all the comings and goings
at the late-night chemist in Wynberg.

My closest friends were cheering me on
when Richard belted me at my grading
and gave me my first black eye.

But now that building's dust and memories,
its red pillars knocked down long ago
and its windows broken like promises.

Reckonings come in strange guises, I guess.
Just this photo of friends – Sharon and Romy,
Natalie and me – is left to tell the story

of the ladies of Chut Sing Tong Long.

Lanterns

Two girls in sandals
calling themselves
'Flower' and 'Plum'
sold me these lanterns –

this cream brocade,
that fine red silk;
taut skin of heaven
and delicate light.

Girls with ponytails,
kids on bikes –
all of them smiling
sweetly at me

as Plum and Flower,
carefully wrapping
the folded lanterns,
revealed their dreams:

a house by the river,
a fruit-bearing garden,
and someday going
to sightsee in

Ho Chi Minh City.

Extinction

The Javan Tiger
disappeared
in the 1970s, in a forest
that could no longer contain it.

The usual reasons
were given: reduced
habitat, civil unrest, prey
species lost to disease.

In this last photograph –
black and white, grainy –
muscle and purpose
are framed as loss.

It joins the others
that won't come back:
Zanzibar Leopard, Chinese
Paddlefish, Guam Flying Fox.

Time's little sketch
on a screen, a disposable
image: eyes like black holes,
stripes like cage bars.

The Pantanal

~ *Matto Grosso, Brazil*

The lilac sky of the Pantanal
invites you to remember.

Deer and jaguar meet in your mind,
a painting by Rousseau.

Water lilies like dinner plates.
Flash of crimson macaw.

The *pantaneiro* will take you
to the blooming interior wall

to see beyond your dreams.
Nightjar over the dark lake

drinks in the cries unchanged
since before the human dumb-show.

Homestead

She imagines her future in this broken house,
the roof just holding as hail shears down.

The borehole's covered and the pillars break
to rubble as water leaks away like light.

Still, she imagines, it will get better.
Animals will pass and the silence will heal.

In a place where the river should start but doesn't,
she lies down close to the soil, where the heat

can be absorbed and then outwaited.
Low stars settle, fat as ticks on her hands.

The Nameless Town

What endures when hills become a smudge
on someone's horizon? When the roads
go off into the veld and disappear?

What becomes of people, places, animals,
when the rind of time is slowly peeled back
like an old ticker-tape that's full of grime

and shadow? Some towns die – not every 'here'
becomes a 'somewhere'. Soil may be a grave,
a scent of loss beneath your fingernails.

That nameless town used to be a wedge
against a wilderness of nosing leopards.
Now it shudders very slowly where

the tractors stopped and new walls fell.
Ploughshares lie in cavernous spaces
where sound has gone, as from a cracked bell.

Driving to the Mountains

What's it like to be born
at the edge of grass and silence?
Just a few kilometres back
are malls, well-knuckled roads,
the obligatory handfuls of people.

On open tracts over the hill,
rows of aloes are flattened in dust
like red armadillos.
The horizon is marked
by posts on a fence.

Farms begin where double doors open.
A hot breeze lifts
the roadside's ragged skirts.
Hours later, the tar
unhands a vision of mountains far

and near, mottled
but grooved and carved
with light,
giving off sparks
like the white burst of the Pleiades

illuminating things gone dark.

The Lemon Farm

We stayed for weeks on a farm in the valley,
watching the empty swimming pool fill
with falling leaves. Birds from the hills
flew down to feast from trays in the trees

and alight on the statues lining the garden
(blindingly white, supposedly Greek).
The terrace shone with polish one morning
as bobbles of bright flamboyant seeds

rained on the slabs of crazy paving
among gouged remnants of prickly pears.
We savoured the smell of autumn's turning,
established our equilibrium there.

The silent sheen of perfect lemons
reflected a light that couldn't break us –
the memories linger (I can't erase them)
of all the mornings that couldn't unmake us.

Mission

~ for Adriana Marais

I've met a woman who's possibly going
to Mars and there's a part of me
that gets the need – that sense of purpose
way beyond kids, degrees, the big house
furnished with bikes and ferns;

the need to be greater than what's beneath
one's skin: a strip-search of one's motives,
just to uncover what it is
that can't be lost or traded. Flight
is always appealing – who would stay

when the flared horizon's opening up
to vapour and silence? It's no longer
Aurora Borealis, but time
itself the field where winged and luminous
insects fly around in the kind

of future I want to see. The need
to explore is like that urge to run
your finger over a canvas by Bosch
or Bruegel: feel what that varnished patch
of time can offer that isn't 'now'.

I have a sense that all these things –
the silence, the lure – are features I can't
ignore; I study their gravity,
and want to understand them soon
so I, too, can complete my mission.

The Townhouse

Home from work, with winter's early
evening cold already frosting
breath, her father said, *Come on,
let's take a walk.* On the long
suburban block, they started out
towards factories and open veld,
blackjacks leaping onto their socks,
cosmos turning small magenta
faces to them as they passed
the barbed wire, wraiths of trees.
They talked a lot – philosophy –
and she would tell him all about
the hell of school. Walking fast,
they always cut across the evening's
early dark and made it home
before the streetlights flickered on.
Her mother served them vegetable
soup with oven-toasted bread
and while she did her homework,
her parents chatted.
                    Now all she has
are memories of the solemn hours
of childhood spent as one of three
in a townhouse in the open veld
surrounded by the growing world
of mine dumps, wire, death and fear
but, all the same, a sanctuary.

Highveld Grass

Hills unfold along the creases
of the map. We play a game –
rock, paper, scissors – in the car;
the destination is so far
and hours are long. Life contracts
to sameness on a dusty trip.

Looking back, I see acacias
furred with yellow and a strip
of eucalyptus trees in shadow.
Breathing in the pungent air,
we stop a while to stretch our legs
and run our fingers through our hair.

On we go. The chunks of rock
and scruffy veld keep coming like
a river. Thirsty, tired and hot,
we long for lollies, one more stop.
My sister yawns. I fold into
my silence, a forget-me-not.

Now, my father's gone; my mother's
going blind. The sun still pierces
T-shirts like it always did.
The Highveld's still a dried-out place
of burning wonder, and I want
to crush its grass against my face.

Acknowledgements

Thanks are due to the editors of the following journals in whose pages versions of some of these poems first appeared: *Five Points, Illuminations, Incwadi, Prufrock, Stanzas, New Contrast: The South African Literary Journal* and *The Johannesburg Review of Books*.

For their advice and support, thanks are also due to Douglas Reid Skinner and my PhD (Creative Writing) supervisor, David Medalie.

Fiona Zerbst

Notes on Epigraphs/Quotations

Phrases, epigraphs and quotations have been used, sometimes with and sometimes without acknowledgement from the following sources:

Page 31
The Tasmanian tiger or thylacine is one of the most fabled animals in the world.
The quotation from the Tasmania Parks & Wildlife Service is found on their website: **www.parks.tas.gov.au**

Page 51
Therefore, don't despair if you see death. Nothing really dies.
Ben Okri, *Astonishing the Gods* (House of Zeus, 2015)

People! Read Poetry

Printed in the United States
By Bookmasters